This journal belongs to

_____

_____

Journals to Write In

Special Interests Publishing

SUGAR LAND, TEXAS

Journals to Write In

Special Interests Publishing
Sugar Land, Texas
www.sipub.com

Ordering Information:
Quantity sales.
Special discounts are available on quantity purchases by corporations, associations, and others. For details, contact the "Special Sales Department" at the address above.

Canadian Women Timeline

~~When women could vote~~

1918 - some women granted
right to vote

1929 - Women declared
1951   as persons

✓ 1960 - All women given
right to vote

1971 - Canadian labour
1985   code was amended
prohibiting discrimination
based on sex & marital
status — equal pay for
equal work

1981 - rights added to
Canadian Charter of
Rights & Freedoms

The Four Agreements

- Stay engaged
- Experience discomfort
- Expect a accept non
  disclosure
- Speak your truth

Why read 21 truths

Find ways to address
myths & misconceptions
Learn more about
Indeginous Peoples & Issues

About
Journals to Write In

Journals to Write In is an imprint of Special Interests Publishing. In addition to our line of useful and fun journals, Special Interests publishes a variety of books, ebooks and courses designed to help you reach your goals and improve your life.

To see what we are up to, visit us online at
https://sipub.com/journals

To learn about other journals available from us, check out
https://amazon.com/author/journals/

We welcome your input and suggestions for new journals or improvements to our journal line. Drop us a line at
journals@sipub.com

Made in the USA
Middletown, DE
23 August 2021